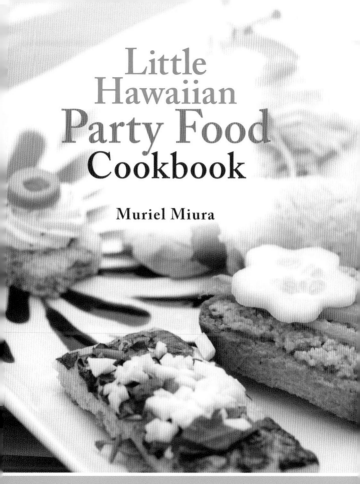

Little Hawaiian Party Food Cookbook

Muriel Miura

MUTUAL PUBLISHING

ISBN-10: 1-56647-848-0
ISBN-13: 978-1-56647-848-9

Photographs by Kaz Tanabe
Design by Wanni

First Printing, September 2007
1 2 3 4 5 6 7 8 9

Mutual Publishing, LLC
1215 Center Street, Suite 210
Honolulu, Hawai'i 96816
Ph: 808-732-1709 / Fax: 808-734-4094
email: info@mutualpublishing.com
www.mutualpublishing.com

Printed in Korea

TABLE OF CONTENTS

INTRODUCTION

Wouldn't you like to fall under the spell of what Mark Twain once called "the loveliest fleet of islands to be anchored in any ocean?" Treat your guests to a taste of paradise the next time you host a pūpū party and serve some of the exotic culinary treasures of Hawai'i. This island state still evokes images of exotic beauty and escape. Unforgettable are the lively memories of the beautiful scenery, poetic music, the hospitable people, the dances, and the exotic foods.

The elaborate pūpū or *hors d'oeuvre* tray one finds at any Island gathering symbolizes the harmony and fusion of the culinary arts of the various peoples of Hawai'i—Stuffed Lychees, Chutney Guacamole, Teriyaki Shrimp, Aloha Punch, Spring Rolls, and Crispy Shrimp Won Ton. The magic of Hawai'i can be in your home with Poke Aku, Taegu, Temaki Sushi, Artichoke Clam Puffs, and Guava Daiquiri! These are but a sampling of recipes that are found in this book.

Many recipes are classic family favorites while others are more contemporary. Throughout it all, the essence of aloha is captured. The recipes also demonstrate the blending of many cuisines.

Here at last in this book are dishes that can transform your next party into a fascinating taste of adventure and give new dimension to your daily meal. It is a book filled with a treasury of exotic-sounding but easy-to-prepare recipes using ingredients that are available in most supermarkets or Asian grocery stores.

You will find mouth-watering recipes from the world's most fascinating islands divided into categories of "Snacks, Chips 'N Dips," "Sushi Treats," "Cold Pūpū," "Hot Pūpū," and "Thirst Quenchers"to make them easier to find. As you cook your way through the pages of *Little Hawaiian Party Food Cookbook*, you will find that cooking Hawaiian-style is a blend of many different cuisines. We hope that you'll have fun preparing many of these fast and easy pūpū, and that you embrace this book as an expression of friendship and aloha from Hawai'i. Enjoy!

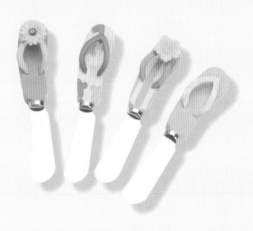

SNACKS,
CHIPS 'N DIPS

Chutney Guacamole

Makes about 5 cups

4 ripe avocados, peeled and seeded
1/3 cup chutney
2 cloves garlic
2 lemons, juiced
Salt and pepper to taste
1 cup chopped tomato

Place avocado, chutney, garlic, and lime juice in blender
jar; blend 2 seconds. Season to taste and add chopped
tomato; blend additional 4 seconds or until
of desired consistency. Chill and serve with corn or
potato chips.

Breadfruit Chips

Serves 4 to 6

1 large firm-ripe breadfruit, about 2 to 3 pounds
1 quart canola oil for deep frying
Salt to taste

Peel breadfruit. Wash under cold water and dry. Cut into four sections and remove core then slice thinly. Deep-fry breadfruit slices in oil heated to 365°F until golden brown. Drain on absorbent paper and salt immediately. Cool. Store chips in air-tight container until ready for use.

VARIATION: Potato or Japanese Taro Chips

Use 1 potato or Japanese taro. Peel and cut potato or taro into paper-thin slices. Soak in cold salted water overnight in refrigerator, and prepare as above.

TIP
Breadfruit Chips freeze well. Defrost at room temperature for about 30 minutes and re-heat in warm oven before serving.

Curried Crudité Dip

Makes about 3 cups

2 cups mayonnaise
1/2 cup sour cream
1/4 teaspoon turmeric
1-1/2 tablespoons curry powder
1 clove garlic, finely minced
1 tablespoon sugar
1/2 teaspoon salt
1 tablespoon fresh lemon juice
2 tablespoons minced parsley

Blend all ingredients together. Chill for 5 to 6 hours or overnight. Serve with crudités.

SUGGESTIONS FOR CRUDITÉS
Carrots, celery, cherry tomatoes, mushrooms, broccoli, cauliflower, and zucchini.

Macadamia Dip

Serves about 12

1 package (8 oz.) cream cheese, softened
2 tablespoons milk
1 jar (2-1/2 oz.) dried chipped beef, shredded
1/4 cup finely minced green pepper
1/2 teaspoon garlic salt
1/4 teaspoon pepper
1 teaspoon onion flakes
1-1/2 teaspoons prepared horseradish
1/2 cup sour cream
1/2 cup macadamia nut bits

Blend cream cheese and milk together. Stir in chopped beef, green pepper, seasonings, onion flakes, and horseradish. Fold in sour cream and spoon into shallow baking dish. Sprinkle nuts over mixture and bake at 350°F for 20 minutes. Serve hot with crackers or chips.

Smoked Salmon Pâté

Makes about 2 cups

1 can (15-1/2 oz.) salmon, drained and flaked
1 package (8 oz.) cream cheese, softened
1 tablespoon lemon or lime juice
2 teaspoons coarsely-grated onion
2 teaspoons prepared horseradish
1/4 teaspoon liquid smoke
2–3 drops hot sauce
1 tablespoon fresh minced parsley

Combine all ingredients except parsley; stir to mix well.
Cover and chill 4 to 6 hours or longer; garnish with
minced parsley just before serving. Great with Melba
or bread rounds of choice.

Shrimp Dip

Serves 10 to 12

1 package (8 oz.) cream cheese, softened
3 tablespoons chili sauce
1 teaspoon finely minced onion
1/2 cup mayonnaise
1 teaspoon lemon juice
1/4 teaspoon Worcestershire sauce
1/2 pound tiny cooked shrimp

Beat cream cheese until smooth; add chili sauce, onion, mayonnaise, lemon juice, and Worcestershire sauce; mix well. Fold in shrimp and serve with toast points or elegant crackers.

Hawaiian Party Mix

Makes about 7 quarts

1 pound butter
1 teaspoon garlic powder
1 cup sugar
2 tablespoons Worcestershire sauce
2 boxes (16 to 18 oz. each) dry cereal (bite-sized
    shredded rice, corn or whole grain squares,
    o-shaped puffed cereal, etc.)
1 can (10 oz.) macadamia nuts
1 package (9 oz.) thin pretzel sticks

Heat butter, garlic powder, sugar, and Worcestershire
sauce in small saucepan until sugar dissolves. Mix
together cereals, nuts, and pretzels in large roasting
pan; pour butter mixture over and mix well. Bake
at 250°F for 1-1/2 hours or until cereals are dry and
crispy, mixing every 15 to 20 minutes. Cool and store
in airtight container.

SUSHI
TREATS

Basic Sushi Rice
Vinegared Rice

Makes about 40 cups Sushi Rice /
About 2 quarts Sushi Rice Vinegar

Awase Zu (Sushi Rice Vinegar)
3-1/4 cups Japanese rice vinegar
1/4 cup mirin (sweetened rice wine)
4-1/2 cups sugar (decrease if desired)
1/4 cup salt

Hot cooked rice, as desired

Combine Awase Zu ingredients in non-reactive saucepan
then heat over low heat until sugar and salt dissolve. Cool.
Pour Sushi Vinegar over hot rice; toss gently to mix while
cooling rice. Do not mix in circular motion. Cool quickly
to retain vinegar flavor and to give rice a glossy sheen.
Use Sushi Rice to make various types of sushi.

TIP
Use about 1 cup Sushi Rice Vinegar to 5 cups of
cooked rice. Cook only enough rice you will need
for one time use. As recipe makes about 2 quarts of
Sushi Rice Vinegar, save remaining vinegar mixture
in covered glass jar in refrigerated or cool place.

Teppo Maki Sushi
Sushi with Pickled Radish
Makes about 32

4 sheets sushi nori (laver), cut into halves
1 piece long takuwan (pickled radish), cut into 8 strips
4 cups prepared Sushi Rice (see page 18)

Place sheet of nori on bamboo mat; spread with about
1/2 cup Sushi Rice, leaving 1-inch uncovered at farthest
end. Place strip of takuwan 1-inch from nearest edge. Roll
away from you, holding takuwan in place with fingers,
lifting mat when it touches rice; continue rolling until
takuwan is completely encased. Squeeze gently and
press ends within mat. Cut each roll into halves; then
diagonally into halves again. Arrange, cut side up, on
serving platter. Serve with Soy Sauce–Wasabi Dip
(see page 26).

VARIATION: Kappa Maki Sushi
Spread wasabi paste lengthwise on middle of Sushi
Rice; substitute cucumber strips for takuwan.

VARIATION: Tekka Maki Sushi
Prepare as above; substitute fresh raw fish fillet strips
for takuwan.

Nigiri Sushi
Finger Sushi
Makes about 2 dozen

1 tablespoon wasabi paste
1 teaspoon water
8 cooked jumbo shrimp, shelled, deveined, and seasoned
8 slices raw sashimi quality fish (aku, 'ahi, 'ōpakapaka,
    sea bass, etc.)
8 slices cooked octopus
4 cups prepared Sushi Rice (see page 18)

Mix together wasabi and water to make thick paste; set aside. Cut shrimp into lengthwise halves. Mold rice into thumb-sized oval mound, about 2 × 1 × 1–inch in size. Dab a little wasabi paste on center of rice and on underside of shrimp, fish, and octopus; place on rice mound. Serve with Soy Sauce–Wasabi Dip (see page 26).

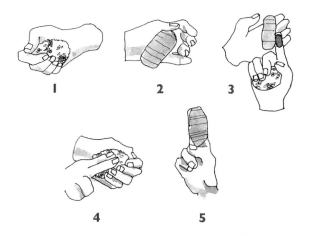

Illustrations by Paul Konishi

Temaki Sushi
Hand-Rolled Sushi

Makes about 20

10 sheets sushi nori (laver, cut into halves)
9 cups Sushi Rice

Fillings
1 avocado, cut into strips and sprinkled with lemon juice
1 Japanese cucumber, cut into strips
1 package kaiware (white radish sprouts), roots removed
Fresh raw fish fillet ('ahi, hamachi), cut into 3-inch strips
Unagi (seasoned eel)
Smoked salmon
Tobiko (flying fish roe)
King crab or imitation crab sticks, cut into strips

Arrange all ingredients attractively on a large tray.
To make Temaki Sushi, use 1/2 sheet of nori for each
serving. Place nori in palm of hand; spoon about
1/4 cup Sushi Rice in center of nori and spread
crosswise at a slight angle. Spread a little wasabi paste
along center of rice; lay Filling(s) of choice on top of
rice. Wrap nori around filling, starting at lower end of
nori and rolling at a slight angle into cone or cylinder
shape. Serve with Soy Sauce–Wasabi Dip (see page 26).

VARIATION: Hawaiian Roll
Spread mayonnaise over wasabi paste on Sushi Rice;
arrange cucumber strip, kaiware, fish strip; roll at a
slight angle to form cone shape.

VARIATION: California Roll
Prepare as for Hawaiian Roll, except arrange cucumber
and avocado strips, crab meat; roll at a slight angle into
cone shape or cylinder. Serve with soy sauce as dip.

Tuna Pan Sushi

Makes about 30 pieces

12 cups prepared Sushi Rice or hot steamed rice

Condiments
2 cans (6 oz. each) tuna, drained
2 tablespoons mirin (sweetened rice wine)
1/4 cup sugar
1/4 cup soy sauce
Fried egg strips
Red or green oboro (dried shrimp flakes)

Beni shoga (pickled red ginger), optional
30 sheets seasoned nori (laver) squares

Stir-fry tuna, mirin, sugar, and soy sauce for 1-2 minutes, stirring constantly. Set aside to cool. Line 9 × 13–inch pan with waxed paper. Sprinkle shrimp flakes evenly in pan. Sprinkle with egg strips then with seasoned tuna. Top with Sushi Rice or plain rice; cover with waxed paper and press down firmly. Cool. Invert on serving tray to serve; cut into 30 pieces; garnish with beni shoga. If desired, place sushi on seasoned nori squares when serving.

Oshi/Cocktail Sushi
Molded Sushi
Makes about 24

4 cups prepared Sushi Rice (see page 18)

Condiments
Red or green oboro (dried shrimp flakes)
Toasted sesame seeds
Fried egg strips or small squares
Minced parsley

Press Sushi Rice into miniature muffin tins or sushi mold; invert from muffin tins to unmold. Cover with moist cloth until ready to serve. Sprinkle top of each with choice of Condiment(s) before serving.

If sushi mold is used: arrange desired condiments on rice; press down and remove mold. Arrange sushi on platter lined with ti leaves and garnished with orchids or parsley.

OSHIWAKU—wooden mold for making pressed or molded sushi.

Illustration by Paul Konishi

Soy Sauce–Wasabi Dip

Serves 1 to 2 persons

1 tablespoon wasabi (powdered horseradish)
1 teaspoon water
Soy sauce

Mix together wasabi and water to make smooth paste.
Place wasabi paste in small condiment dish; add desired
amount of soy sauce and stir to mix well. Excellent as
dip for sushi and sashimi.

TIPS
- 1 cup of uncooked rice will yield 3 cups of cooked rice.
- Ready-to-use wasabi paste in tubes may be found in
  the Asian food section of supermarkets.

COLD PŪPŪ

Artichoke Balls

Makes about 4 dozen

1 clove garlic, finely minced
2 tablespoons olive oil
2 cans (8 oz. each) artichoke hearts, drained and chopped
2 eggs, slightly beaten
1/4 teaspoon cayenne
3/4 cup grated Parmesan cheese
3/4 cup dry bread crumbs

Sauté garlic in oil, but do not allow it to brown. Add artichoke, eggs, and cayenne; cook over low heat 5 minutes. Remove from heat; set aside. Combine Parmesan cheese with bread crumbs; mix well. Add 1 cup cheese mixture to artichoke mixture; mix then form into walnut-size balls; dredge in remaining cheese-bread crumbs mixture. Chill and serve.

TIP
A tray of canapés is a beautiful beginning for any party. Cut bread into intriguing shapes; spread with "butter," then filling of your choice, and decorate gaily.

Boiled Peanuts

Makes 5 pounds

5 pounds raw peanuts in shells
1 cup Hawaiian rock salt
4 pieces star anise
2 tablespoons sugar
1/4 cup mirin (sweetened rice wine)

Rinse peanuts; place in large pot with enough water to cover. Add salt, star anise, sugar, and mirin. Cover and bring to a boil; lower heat and simmer 1 hour. After 1 hour, taste-test peanut to see if done but still crisp. Turn heat off and let stand until water cools to room temperature. Drain and serve.

TIP
Convert your large mixing bowl into an attractive punch bowl by encircling the bowl with wire mesh. Insert flower stems into the wire openings; secure in place with toothpicks. Place bowl on "bed" of greenery.

Spicy Warabi
Fern Shoots
Serves 8 to 10

1 bunch warabi (fern shoots or fiddleheads)
1 package (3 oz.) dried codfish, softened in water
    and shredded
1 block kamaboko (fish cake), julienned
1 Shio-fuki kombu (dried salted seaweed)
1 teaspoon sesame oil
Dash shichimi togarashi (chili powder)

Clean and wash warabi. Cut into bite-size pieces and parboil. Drain well and add codfish, kamaboko, and kombu. Add sesame oil; toss to mix ingredients well. Refrigerate before serving.

TIP
Warabi (Fiddleheads), the coiled tips of young fern, have a delicate flavor often described as a cross between asparagus and woodsy mushrooms.

Tofu Poke
Soybean Curd Appetizer
Serves 6 to 8

1 block firm tofu, drained and cut in 1-inch cubes
1 teaspoon toasted sesame seeds
1/4 cup coarsely chopped limu (seaweed), washed
    and cleaned
2 tablespoons minced green onion
1 teaspoon grated fresh ginger root
1 small Hawaiian red chili pepper, seeded and chopped
1/4 cup soy sauce
2 teaspoons sesame oil

Drain cubed tofu in colander then place in serving
bowl. Sprinkle sesame seeds, limu, green onion,
ginger, and chili pepper over tofu; toss gently to mix.
Mix together soy sauce with sesame oil; pour over tofu
mixture and toss lightly. Chill 1 hour before serving.

Stuffed Lychees

Makes about 15

1 package (3 oz.) cream cheese, softened
1/2 cup minced macadamia nuts
1 can (11 oz.) lychee, drained

Combine cream cheese and macadamia nuts; mix well.
Stuff cheese mixture into lychee cavity. Chill before
serving.

Beef Jerky Tasters

Serves 6 to 10

1 package (8 oz.) cream cheese, softened
1 teaspoon prepared horseradish
1 package (2 oz.) beef jerky, minced

Combine cream cheese with horseradish; mix to blend well. Form into small balls; roll and press balls in beef jerky to coat. Chill 1 hour; insert cocktail picks to serve.

TIPS ON PINEAPPLE CUTTING:
Outrigger Style
1. Cut pineapple into quarters, leaving crown on.
2. Loosen fruit by cutting under the core but without removing it. Also cut close to rind.
3. Remove fruit and cut crosswise.
4. Replace fruit in shell in staggered arrangement.

Illustration by Jenna Sakai

Dried Teriyaki Fish

Makes about 1-1/2 pounds

2-1/2 pounds fish fillet, cut into 1/4-inch thick strips
2 teaspoons toasted sesame seeds

Marinade
1 cup soy sauce
3/4 cup sugar
1/4 cup water
1 teaspoon sake (rice wine) or sherry
2 cloves garlic, crushed
1/2 teaspoon canola oil
1 teaspoon minced fresh ginger root

Combine Marinade ingredients in resealable plastic bag; shake to mix thoroughly. Marinate fish strips overnight. Drain. Sprinkle with sesame seeds and screen-dry in hot sun one day or in oven at 200°F for 3 to 4 hours or until of "jerky" texture. Slice to serve.

Taegu
Seasoned Codfish
Serves 6 to 8

1 package (3 oz.) dried cod or cuttlefish*, shredded
1 teaspoon toasted sesame seeds
1 teaspoon paprika
1/4 teaspoon chopped Hawaiian red chili pepper
1/3 cup honey
1 tablespoon soy sauce
1-1/2 teaspoons sesame oil
1/3 teaspoon garlic salt

Soak fish in water 15 to 30 minutes; pat dry and shred; set aside. Combine remaining ingredients in a jar; cover and shake to mix. Add codfish, cover and shake again to distribute seasonings evenly. Refrigerate for 3 days before serving.

TIP
*Shredded cuttlefish may be found in most Asian grocery stores and occasionally in the Asian food section of supermarkets.

Teriyaki Shrimp

Serves 15 to 20

1-1/2 pounds large shrimp (15-20) in the shell
1/3 cup soy sauce
1/3 cup water
1/3 cup mirin (sweetened rice wine)
1/4 cup sugar
1 tablespoon chopped fresh ginger root
1 teaspoon dashi-no-moto (soup stock base), optional
2 tablespoons minced green onion

Rinse shrimp under cold running water; set aside.
Combine remaining ingredients except green onion in
large saucepan; bring to a boil. Add shrimp; cook over
medium heat until just pink and opaque throughout,
about 2 to 3 minutes. May be served in the shell, or shell
and devein 1 hour before serving. Garnish with minced
green onion.

Poke Aku or 'Ahi
Raw Tuna Appetizer
Serves 8 to 12

2 pounds fresh raw aku or 'ahi fillet, cubed
1 cup limu (seaweed), cleaned and chopped
Hawaiian rock salt to taste
1 small Hawaiian red chili pepper, seeded and minced
1 teaspoon sesame oil or hot chili oil
Kukui 'Inamona (kukui nut paste) to taste, optional

Combine fish with limu, tossing gently to mix well. Add remaining ingredients; toss gently to mix. Chill to serve.

VARIATION: Korean-style Poke
Combine soy sauce, minced ginger, minced green onion, thin slices of sweet Maui onions, and Hawaiian red chili pepper to taste; toss with raw fish fillet cubes.

Spicy Crab Claws

Serves 15 to 20

3 pounds cooked crab claws
1 cup minced green onion
1/4 cup chopped parsley
2 cloves garlic, mashed
3/4 cup extra virgin olive oil
1/2 cup tarragon vinegar
3 tablespoons lemon juice
1 tablespoon Worcestershire sauce
Dash of hot pepper sauce
Salt and freshly ground pepper to taste

If cooked crab claws are frozen, thaw, wash, and drain before using. Place crab in large bowl. Heat remaining ingredients in saucepan; pour over crab; cover and refrigerate overnight. Remove from refrigerator 1 hour before serving; drain. Serve with buttered black or rye bread.

King Clam Poke

Serves 8 to 12

1 small king clam, cleaned (use nozzle and breast only)
1/4 cup minced green onion
1 medium sweet Maui onion, thinly sliced
2 teaspoons hot chili oil
2 tablespoons toasted sesame seeds
1 tablespoon soy sauce or Hawaiian rock salt to taste

Immerse clam in boiling water to cover for 1 minute.
Peel off outer skin and slice into thin diagonal slices.
Place clam in bowl; add remaining ingredients and
toss gently to mix. Chill to serve.

HOT PŪPŪ

Artichoke Clam Puffs

Makes about 36

2 packages (9 oz. each) frozen artichoke heart halves
1 package (8 oz.) cream cheese, softened
1 tablespoon minced onion
2 tablespoons fresh lemon juice
1/4 teaspoon hot pepper sauce
1 can (6-1/2 oz.) minced clams, drained

Cook artichoke hearts according to package directions; drain and arrange, cut-sides up, on greased or non-stick baking sheet. Combine cream cheese, onion, lemon juice, and hot pepper sauce; stir in clams. Spoon mixture onto artichokes; sprinkle with paprika. Bake at 400°F 10 to 12 minutes or until lightly browned and bubbly.

QUICK 'N EASY PŪPŪ
Bake smoked oyster or small sausage in pastry or phyllo.

Artichoke Squares

Serves 10 to 12

1 jar (6 oz.) marinated artichoke hearts
1/2 cup minced onion
1 clove garlic, finely minced
4 eggs, beaten
1/4 cup dry bread crumbs
1/4 teaspoon salt
Dash of pepper
Dash of oregano
Dash of chili powder
2 tablespoons minced parsley
1-1/2 cups grated cheddar cheese

Drain liquid from one jar of artichoke hearts into skillet. Chop artichokes and set aside. Cook onion and garlic in artichoke liquid; set aside. In a large bowl, mix together eggs, bread crumbs, salt, pepper, oregano, chili powder, and parsley. Stir in cheese. Add artichokes and onion-garlic mixture. Pour into greased 7 × 11–inch pan. Bake at 325°F for 30 minutes. Cool in pan and cut into bite-size pieces to serve. Delicious served warm.

Beef Lettuce Wrap

Serves 6 to 8

2 tablespoons canola oil
2 cloves garlic, finely minced
1 pound coarsely ground lean beef
1 tablespoon curry powder
1/2 cup finely minced onion
1/2 teaspoon salt
Lettuce leaves
Mint leaves

Heat oil and sauté garlic. Add meat, curry powder, celery and seasonings; cook 3 to 5 minutes, stirring occasionally. To serve, place in bowl surrounded by lettuce leaves. Have guests put a spoonful of meat mixture into lettuce leaf, add mint leaf, and fold to eat. This is a fun dish when entertaining a small group.

VARIATION:
Substitute lean ground pork, turkey, or chicken.

Teriyaki Sausage

Serves about 10 to 12

2 pounds Portuguese sausage or dinner franks,
    cut into 1/2-inch slices
3/4 cup sugar
1/4 cup mirin (sweetened rice wine)
3/4 cup soy sauce
1/2 teaspoon grated fresh ginger root

Stir-fry sausage in non-stick skillet 1 to 2 minutes.
Stir in remaining ingredients, cover and simmer
sausage 10 to 15 minutes over low heat or until sauce
is almost completely absorbed. Serve hot with decorative
wooden picks.

QUICK 'N EASY PŪPŪ
Wrap cocktail onions in 1/2 strips of bacon; fasten
with colored pick; broil and serve hot.

Easy Char Siu Bao

Makes 12

1 can (10.2 oz.) refrigerated Parkerhouse rolls or biscuits

Filling
1 cup char siu (sweet roast pork), chopped
2 tablespoons minced green onion
1/2 teaspoon soy sauce
Dash of pepper

2 tablespoons canola oil

Combine Filling ingredients and mix thoroughly. Place 1 tablespoon filling in center of each circle of dough. Pinch edges of dough together to seal. Brush top of each bao with salad oil. Steam in waxed paper-lined steamer for 15 to 20 minutes.

VARIATION: Baked Char Siu Bao
Follow directions on the can of the refrigerated Parkerhouse rolls or biscuits for baking.

QUICK 'N EASY PŪPŪ
Wrap thick banana slices, which have been soaked in lemon juice, in 1/2 strips of bacon; fasten with colored pick; broil until brown on all sides. Serve hot.

Kamaboko Tempura
Fishcake Fritters

Makes about 40

3/4 cup flour
1/2 teaspoon salt
2 teaspoons sugar
1/2 teaspoon baking powder
1/4 cup ice cold water
6 eggs
1/4 cup minced green onion
1 block kamaboko, coarsely grated

Canola oil for frying

Combine flour, salt, sugar, and baking powder; blend well. Beat together water and eggs until frothy; add all at once to flour mixture and stir only to moisten dry ingredients. Stir in green onion and kamaboko. Drop by teaspoonfuls into oil heated to 365°F and deep-fry until golden on all sides. Drain on absorbent paper. Ono hot or cold!

QUICK 'N EASY PŪPŪ
Wrap pineapple chunks with bacon; fasten with colored pick and broil until crisp. Serve hot.

Teriyaki Beef Tidbits

Makes about 30 pieces

1 pound sirloin steak, cubed

Sauce
1/2 cup brown sugar, packed
2/3 cup soy sauce
1/4 cup mirin (sweetened rice wine)
1 clove garlic, crushed
1 slice fresh ginger root, crushed

Place meat cubes in skillet or chafing dish. Mix together Sauce ingredients; pour over meat. Cook on low heat 15 to 20 minutes or until done as desired. Serve with decorative wooden picks.

QUICK 'N EASY PŪPŪ
Stuff pitted prune or date with well-drained pineapple tidbit, almond or whole macadamia nut; wrap with half strip of bacon; fasten with colored pick; broil until crisp and serve hot.

Sweet Potato Tempura

Serves 6 to 8

1 medium sweet potato, sliced 1/4-inch thick

Batter
1 cup biscuit mix
1/2 cup flour
1/2 cup cornstarch
1-1/2 cups cold water

1 quart canola oil for frying

Cook sweet potato in salted water 30 to 60 seconds or until tender but firm; drain and set aside. Combine dry ingredients for Batter; mix well; add water all at once and stir only until dry ingredients are moistened (batter may be lumpy). Dip potato slices into batter; deep-fry in oil heated to 365 to 375°F. until delicately browned on both sides. Drain on absorbent paper and serve hot or cold.

Fried Beef Patties
Wan-Jah Juhn
Makes about 30 to 36

1 pound lean ground beef

Seasonings
2 tablespoons soy sauce
1/2 teaspoon salt
Dash of pepper
2 tablespoons minced green onion
2 tablespoons toasted, crushed sesame seeds
1/4 teaspoon minced fresh ginger root
1 large clove garlic, finely minced

1/3 cup flour
3 eggs, slightly beaten
1/4 cup canola oil for frying

Combine beef with seasonings and mix well. Form into small patties, 1/2-inch in diameter. Dip first in flour, then in beaten egg, again in flour, and finally in beaten egg. Pan-fry in hot oil until lightly browned, 1 to 2 minutes on each side. Drain on absorbent paper.

Dip patties in sauce made by combining 3 tablespoons soy sauce, 1 tablespoon rice vinegar, and 1 teaspoon finely minced green onion to serve, if desired.

Shiitake Mushroom Turnovers

Makes about 4 dozen

Pastry
1 package (8 oz.) cream cheese, softened
1/2 pound butter, softened
2 cups sifted flour
1 egg yolk
2 teaspoons cream or milk

Filling
1/2 pound fresh shiitake mushrooms, sliced
1 small onion, finely minced
1/4 cup butter
2 teaspoons flour
1/2 teaspoon salt
1/2 cup sour cream

To make Pastry, combine cheese and butter. Work
in flour until a smooth dough is formed; cover and
refrigerate 2 hours. In a separate bowl, mix together egg
yolk and cream; set aside.

To prepare Filling, sauté mushrooms and onion in
butter. Add flour and salt; cook 1 to 2 minutes; remove
from heat and stir in sour cream. Roll dough 1/8-inch
thick on lightly floured surface; cut into 3-inch circles.
Place about 1 teaspoon filling just off-center of each
dough circle; fold in half and press edges together.

Seal with fork tines. Place turnovers on baking pan
lightly sprayed with oil. Brush tops of pastry with egg
yolk–cream mixture. Bake at 375°F for 15 to 20 minutes
or until golden brown. May be served hot or cold.

TIP
This freezes well for later use.

Crispy Pork Won Ton
Fried Pork Dumplings

Makes about 30 to 36

Filling

3/4 pound lean ground pork
1/4 cup water chestnuts, minced
2 tablespoons minced green onion
1 egg, slightly beaten
1 tablespoon soy sauce
1 teaspoon salt
1 teaspoon sugar

1 package won ton wrappers*
1 quart canola oil for frying

Mix together all ingredients for Filling. Place 1 teaspoon filling in center of won ton wrapper. Fold into desired shape, moisten edges with water and pinch together to seal. Fry won ton in oil heated to 365 to 375°F until golden brown; drain on absorbent paper. If desired, may be served with soy sauce or purchased sweet-sour sauce.

VARIATION: Ham or Luncheon Meat Won Ton
Substitute minced ham or luncheon meat for ground pork.

VARIATION: Shrimp Won Ton
Substitute raw minced shrimp for ground pork.

VARIATION: Tuna Won Ton
Substitute drained can of tuna for ground pork.

TIP
*Won ton wrappers may be found in the refrigerator section of most Asian groceries. Won ton may be made ahead and frozen. Thaw before frying, or fry earlier in the day and reheat before serving.

Lumpia
Spring Rolls
Serves about 25

Filling

1 pound lean ground beef
1/2 cup chopped onion
2 cloves garlic, minced
1/4 pound raw shrimp, cleaned and minced
1/2 cup chopped mushrooms
1/2 cup grated carrot
1/4 cup chopped green onion
2 cups shredded won bok
2 tablespoons soy sauce
Salt and pepper to taste
2 tablespoons flour
1/4 cup water

50 lumpia wrappers
1 quart canola oil for frying

Lumpia Sauce

1/3 cup soy sauce
3 tablespoons lemon juice

In a large skillet, brown beef with onion and garlic.
Add shrimp, vegetables, and seasonings; cook 1 to
2 minutes. Drain and set aside to cool thoroughly.
Combine flour and water to make a paste. Place
2 tablespoons of cooled filling mixture on each lumpia
wrapper. Fold nearest edge of wrapper over filling; fold
left and right sides toward center and roll lightly toward
open end. Seal with flour paste. Fry lumpia in oil
heated to 375°F until golden brown; drain on absorbent
paper and serve with Lumpia Sauce.

Pineapple Teri-bobs

Makes 16 to 18

3/4 pound beef, cut in 3/4-inch cubes
1/2 pound boneless chicken, cut in 3/4-inch cubes
1 package (7 oz.) Portuguese sausage, cut in
    3/4-inch slices
1 can (No. 2) pineapple chunks, drained and
    juice reserved

Marinade
1/2 cup soy sauce
1/2 cup pineapple juice
1 clove garlic, crushed
1/4-inch slice fresh ginger root, crushed

16–18 bamboo or metal skewers (4 to 5 inches long)

Mix together all ingredients for Marinade in large
resealable plastic bag. Add beef, chicken, and
Portuguese sausage; marinate 1 hour. Thread cubes of
meats and pineapple alternately on skewers. Broil 3 to
5 minutes; baste, turn, and baste again with marinade
then broil 5 minutes longer or until done. Serve hot.

TIP
If bamboo skewers are used, soak in water 30 minutes to prevent burning.

Teri Fish Cubes

Serves about 25

3 pounds fish fillet, cubed

Marinade
3/4 cup soy sauce
1/2 cup sugar
1 clove garlic, crushed
2 slices (1/4-inch each) fresh ginger root, crushed
2 tablespoons mirin (sweetened rice wine)

2 eggs, beaten
3 tablespoons water
Flour
2 cups panko or dry bread crumbs
1 quart canola oil for frying

Mix Marinade ingredients together in resealable plastic bag; add fish cubes and marinate 2 hours. Mix together eggs and water; set aside. Drain fish then dredge in flour; dip in egg mixture then coat with panko or bread crumbs. Deep-fry in oil heated to 365 to 375°F until golden. Drain on absorbent paper and serve hot.

Sweet Potato Nibbles

Serves 4 to 6

1 pound sweet potatoes, about 2-inches in diameter
1/4 cup canola or olive oil
1/2 cup sour cream

Toppings
Chopped chives
Caviar
Bacon bits
Chutney

Scrub sweet potatoes; trim ends. Cut into 1/4-inch crosswise slices. Arrange sweet potato slices in single layer on oiled baking sheet. Brush potato tops with remaining oil. Bake at 400°F on first side for 15 minutes; turn and bake additional 10 minutes or until golden brown on second side. Top each slice with sour cream and desired Toppings. Serve hot or at room temperature.

Glazed Cocktail Ribs

Serves 12 to 14

1 rack (4 pounds) pork spareribs, sawed in half
   crosswise by butcher

Marinade
1 cup chili sauce
1/4 cup honey
2 tablespoons soy sauce
2 large cloves garlic, crushed

Mix together Marinade ingredients; spread over ribs;
cover and let stand in refrigerator overnight. To cook,
arrange ribs in a single layer on rack of foil-lined
baking pan. Bake, uncovered, at 350°F for 40 to 60
minutes or until done. Cut into individual cocktail-size
pieces to serve. Delicious hot or at room temperature.

Sweet 'N Sour Meatballs

Serves 10

1 pound lean ground beef
1/4 cup water chestnuts
1 clove garlic, minced
1 teaspoon salt
1/2 cup soft bread crumbs
1 teaspoon soy sauce
2 eggs, slightly beaten
1/2 teaspoon pepper

Sauce
1 cup chicken broth
1/2 cup sugar
3 tablespoons cornstarch
1/2 cup pineapple juice, reserved from pineapple chunks
1/2 cup vinegar
2 tablespoons soy sauce
1 green pepper, chopped
1 can (8 oz.) pineapple chunks, drained and juice reserved

In a large bowl, combine ground beef, water chestnuts, garlic, salt, bread crumbs, soy sauce, eggs, and pepper; mix thoroughly. Form into small meatballs; brown in skillet lightly sprayed with oil. Drain on absorbent paper; set aside.

In a saucepan, combine chicken broth, sugar, cornstarch, pineapple juice, vinegar, and soy sauce; cook over medium heat, stirring constantly, for 2 to 3 minutes or until thickened. Add green pepper, pineapple chunks, and meatballs; simmer for additional 5 to 10 minutes over low heat. Place in chafing dish to serve.

Hot Chicken Wings

Serves about 20

4 pounds chicken wings

Seasonings
1 tablespoon cayenne
2 tablespoons paprika
2 tablespoons garlic powder
1 tablespoon dried oregano
2 teaspoons dried thyme leaves
1 tablespoon onion powder
1 tablespoon salt
1 teaspoon freshly ground pepper
1/4 cup olive or canola oil

Remove and discard pointed tip of each wing; separate at joint. Blend all seasonings in food processor or blender until well-mixed. Slowly pour in oil and process until thick paste forms. Combine chicken with spice paste; toss until wings are well-coated. Cover and refrigerate overnight. Broil, turning once, until golden brown outside and cooked through, about 15 to 20 minutes. Serve hot or at room temperature.

TIP
If food processor or blender is not available, wire whisk may be used.

THIRST
QUENCHERS

Aloha Punch

Makes about 20 punch cups

1 can (6 oz.) frozen liliko'i concentrate, thawed
1 can (46 oz.) pineapple juice, chilled
1 can (46 oz.) apricot nectar, chilled
1/4 cup lemon juice

Dilute liliko'i concentrate in punch bowl according to can directions. Add pineapple juice and apricot nectar; mix well; chill and serve over ice.

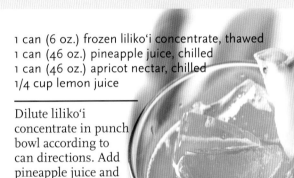

Fruity Slush

Serves 6 to 8

1 can grapefruit sections
1 can mandarin orange
1 can crushed pineapple
1-1/2 cups sugar
Water
1 liter lemon–lime carbonated drink

Mint leaves

Drain fruits; reserve juices. Mash grapefruit and mandarin oranges; set aside. Add water to fruit juices to make 3 cups; dissolve sugar in liquid. Add fruits; mix well, and pour into ice cube trays. Freeze. To serve, crush frozen fruit cubes and place into water glasses; pour lemon–lime carbonated drink over. If desired, garnish with mint.

Frosty Golden Hawaiian Punch

Serves 10 to 12

2 cans (20 oz. each) crushed pineapple in juice, chilled
1 can (6 oz.) frozen lemonade concentrate, thawed
1/4 cup sugar
1 bottle (28 oz.) club soda
1 tray ice cubes

Blend together pineapple with its juice until well-combined and thick. In chilled punch bowl, stir together blended pineapple, lemonade concentrate, and sugar; stir to combine well. Add club soda and ice cubes just before serving.

Guava Daiquiri

Serves 1

1-1/2 ounces light rum
2 ounces guava juice concentrate
1/2 ounce lemon juice
Dash simple syrup
Cracked ice

Garnish with *vanda* or *dendrobium* orchid

Combine all ingredients except orchid in blender; blend on high about 30 seconds or until of slush consistency. Serve in saucer-champagne glass, garnished as desired.

VARIATION: Mango Daiquiri
Substitute 1/4 cup fresh mango chunks for guava concentrate.

VARIATION: Pineapple Daiquiri
Substitute 2 ounces pineapple juice; add pineapple chunk pieces for guava juice.

Soda Freeze

Serves 4 to 6

3 cans (12 oz. each) soda (root beer, coke, orange, or
    strawberry)
1 can (12 oz.) lemon–lime soda
1 can (14 oz.) sweetened condensed milk

Mix 3 cans soda, with 1 can lemon–lime soda and 1 can
condensed milk. Freeze in ice trays. After 2-1/2 to 3
hours, stir every 30 to 45 minutes to aerate the mixture.
Repeat 2 to 4 times until slushy. To serve, mound soda
freeze over vanilla ice cream. Delicious!

TIP
Ice cubes or blocks made with fruit juices or
ginger ale instead of water will prevent the drink
from being diluted. Add your ice garnish to the
punch bowl at the last minute.

Liliko'i–Strawberry Punch

2 pints fresh strawberries
1 can (6 oz.) frozen lemonade concentrate, thawed
1 can (6 oz.) frozen orange juice concentrate, thawed
1 can (6 oz.) frozen liliko'i concentrate, thawed
3 cups ice cold water
1 liter ginger ale, chilled

Wash, hull, and slice strawberries; set aside. Combine remaining ingredients in large punch bowl; stir to combine. Float strawberries in punch to serve.

Champagne Punch

Serves about 25

2 bottles cold champagne
1/2 bottle brandy
2 jiggers Cointreau
1/2 bottle Sauterne, optional
1 bottle (28 oz.) ginger ale, chilled
1/2 bottle (14 oz.) club soda, chilled

Combine all ingredients in a punch bowl; mix well.
Add ring of ice to chill and serve in champagne glasses.

TIP
Cointreau, White Curaçao, and Triple Sec are very
similar. All are prepared from fine spirits with
orange peel as the principal flavor. Cointreau is the
sweetest of the three.

Guava Wine Cooler

Serves 10 to 12

1 quart rosé wine, chilled
3/4 cup guava nectar, chilled
2 tablespoons lemon juice, chilled
1-1/2 cups lemon–lime carbonated drink, chilled

Mint leaves

Combine wine, guava nectar, lemon
juice, and lemon–lime carbonated
drink in punch bowl; mix. Serve
over ice and garnish with mint.

Mock Champagne

Makes about 1 quart

1/2 cup sugar
1/2 cup cold water
1/2 cup grapefruit juice
1/4 cup orange juice
2 cups ginger ale, chilled
3 tablespoons grenadine syrup
Lemon peel

Combine sugar and water in a saucepan; bring to a boil and cook over low heat for about 10 minutes, stirring only until sugar is dissolved. Cool. Add grapefruit and orange juices to simple syrup and chill thoroughly. Just before serving, add ginger ale and grenadine. Add lemon peel. Serve in champagne glasses.

Glossary

A

'Ahi:
Hawaiian tuna fishes, especially the yellow-fin tuna.

Aku:
Bonito, skipjack, an important food.

B

Bean sprouts:
Any of various sprouted beans, especially mung beans or lentils or edible soybeans.

Beni shoga:
A type of Japanese pickle. It is made from ginger cut into thin strips, colored red, and pickled in Umezu.

Breadfruit:
A large, round, starchy fruit native to the Pacific islands; baked or roasted for food.

C

Chinese parsley (or cilantro):
An herb native to Europe, having strong-scented leaves used in cooking.

Chives:
A Eurasian bulbous herb cultivated for its long, slender, hollow leaves.

Chutney:
A sauce or relish of East Indian origin, often composed of both sweet and sour ingredients.

Coconut:
The large, hard-shelled seed of the coconut palm, lined with a white edible meat, and containing a milky liquid.

D

Dashi no moto:
Fish broth/stock granules/powder.

G

Ginger:
The gnarled rhizome of a fall-flowering plant native to China. Available fresh, powdered, pickled, or candied.

Guava:
Tropical fruit, round with yellow skin, pink inner flesh, and many seeds.

H

Hamachi:
Yellowtail tuna.

K

Kaiware:
Radish sprouts.

Kamaboko:
Japanese steamed fishcake.

Kukui 'inamona:
Roasted, pounded, and salted kukui nut.

L

Liliko'i:
Egg-shaped fruit filled with a seedy pulp; passion fruit.

Lychee:
Round, sweet, juicy, white fruit enclosed in a rough, red skin.

M

Macadamia nut:
Rich, slightly sweet nut.

Mango:
Tropical fruit .

Mirin:
Sweetened rice wine.

N

Nori:
Laver; seaweed.

O

Oboro:
Shrimp flakes.

P

Passion fruit:
See Liliko'i.

Portuguese sausage:
Garlic-and-pepper flavored pork sausage.

Panko:
Japanese-style dry bread crumbs.

S

Sake:
Rice wine.

Star anise:
Brownish seeds with eight points—tastes like licorice.

Sashimi:
Raw fish slices; shellfishes and beef are also served raw as sashimi.

Sesame seeds:
Small, flat, oval, white or black seeds used to flavor or garnish foods.

Soy sauce:
A dark salty liquid made from soybeans, flour, salt, and water. Also called shoyu.

Shiitake mushrooms:
Second most cultivated mushroom in the world. Available fresh or dried.

T

Takuwan:
Pickled radish.

Tobiko:
Flying fish roe.

Tofu:
Soybean curd.

U

Unagi:
Eel.

W

Warabi:
Fern sprouts.

Wasabi:
Horseradish.

Wasabi paste:
Combination of wasabi powder and water.

Water chestnuts:
Bulb of an Asian marsh plant.